Introduction to Negotiable Instruments

As Per Indian Laws

By Siva Prasad Bose

Published by Joy Bose

Copyright © 2021 Siva Prasad Bose and Joy Bose

All rights reserved. No part of this book may be reproduced, or stored in a retrieval system, or transmitted in any form or by any means, electronic, mechanical, photocopying, recording, or otherwise, without express written permission of the publisher.

Contents

Preface

Acknowledgments

Chapter 1: What is a Negotiable Instrument

Chapter 2: Historical background of negotiable instruments legislation in Indian law

Chapter 3: Preamble of the Negotiable Instruments Act

Chapter 4: Features and types of Negotiable Instruments

Chapter 5: Characteristics of Bill of Exchange

Chapter 6: Characteristics of Promissory Notes

Chapter 7: Characteristics of Cheques

Chapter 8: Real-World Applications and Modern Developments

Chapter 9: Conclusion

About the author

Glossary of Key Terms

Other books by Siva Prasad Bose

Preface

Negotiable instruments, such as cheques, promissory notes, and bills of exchange, are financial tools that can be transferred between parties. Such instruments are responsible for millions of dollars of financial fraud globally. Therefore, it is important to have some understanding of what they are, and the laws related to them.

In this book, we introduce the concept of negotiable instruments and the laws in India regarding the same, especially the negotiable instruments act and its amendments. We discuss two types of negotiable instruments, promissory notes, and cheques, in more detail.

It is hoped that this book will enable the reader to get an idea of different kinds of negotiable instruments and laws in India related to them.

Acknowledgements

The author is grateful to the following books that were consulted on the topic:

- Khergamvala On The Negotiable Instruments Act As Amended By The Negotiable Instruments (Amendment) Act, 2015. By Khergamvala, LexisNexis, 2017.
- The Negotiable Instruments Act, 1881 - Bare Act with Short Notes. By Lexis, 2020
- The Negotiable Instruments Act (with Case-law on Dishonour of Cheques, Specimen Notices & Complaints). By Bhashyam & Adiga, revised by Shriniwas Gupta. Bharat Law House, New Delhi, 2018

Chapter 1: What is a Negotiable Instrument

In this chapter, we study the definition of a negotiable instrument and its characteristics.

1.1 Definition of negotiable instrument

A negotiable instrument is a signed document that promises to pay the bearer a specified sum of money, either on demand or at a specific time. It can mean a bill of exchange, promissory note or cheque payable either to order or to the bearer (Sec 13, Negotiable instruments act 1881) whether the words "order" or "bearer" appears on the instrument or not, that promises to pay a fixed amount of money without any condition, either on demand or at a future date.

Negotiable instruments are commonly used in all types of business transactions and contracts. It is not necessary that it should be expressly stated to be payable to the order of a person.

The term "negotiable" implies that the instrument can usually be transferred from the payee to a different payee, and so on for any number of times, along with their associated rights. The term "instrument" means that it is written on a piece of paper and not just a verbal promise.

Interest may or may not be added to the amount mentioned on the negotiable instrument.

A negotiable instrument typically has some conditions to be valid: it must be in writing, must be signed by the payer, must have a monetary value, and must create an obligation for payment of a definite sum from one party to another.

The negotiable instruments do not include cash, money orders, deeds, IOUs or letters of credit.

Figure: A Promissory Note from 1939, Rangoon, Burma. Central Bank of India, Public domain, via Wikimedia Commons

Some of the characteristics of negotiable instruments are as follows:

- If a bill or promissory note or a cheque is payable to a particular person and there is nothing to indicate a contrary intention, then it is payable to order and is negotiable.
- If there is anything to indicate that it is not a negotiable instrument but an ordinary actionable claim, the rules relating to negotiable instruments do not apply to it.
- Cheque is only a particular form of bill of exchange drawn on a special banker and payable on demand. The negotiable instruments act, therefore, practically deals with two kinds of instruments, the promissory notes and bills of exchange. The main distinction between the two is that in a promissory note the executant makes the promise himself, while in a bill of exchange he directs a third-party person to pay.

A negotiable instrument is, therefore, an unconditional order or promise to pay an amount of money, easily transferable from one person to another. Example: check, promissory note, draft (bill of exchange).

The uniform commercial code requires that for an instrument to be negotiable, it must be signed by the maker or drawer (and sometimes stamped as well and/or written on stamp paper), and must contain an unconditional promise or order to pay a specific amount of money. It must be payable on demand or at a specified future time and must be payable to order or to the bearer, so it creates a financial obligation.

Negotiable instruments can be applicable within a country such as India or can be international. The United Nations Convention on International Bills of Exchange and International Promissory Notes (New York, 1988) governs negotiable instruments that are applicable for payments internationally.

Negotiable instruments have become integral to modern economies, facilitating secure and efficient financial transactions. In addition to the foundational concepts, the practical applications in credit systems, trade financing, and personal transactions underscore their importance. For instance, a cheque issued as a payment instrument in international trade highlights how negotiable instruments transcend geographical and economic boundaries.

1.2 Characteristics of negotiable instruments

Thomas in his book "Principles of banking" says that: a negotiable instrument is one which is by a legally recognized custom of trade or law, transferable by delivery in such circumstances that:

- The holder of it for the time being may sue on it in his known name
- The property in it passes to a bonafide transferee for value, notwithstanding any deficit of the transferor

According to Bhashyam and Adiga: A negotiable instrument is one, which when transferred by delivery or endorsement and delivery passes to the transferee a good title to payment according to its tenor and irrespective of the title of the transferor.

What is a negotiable instrument?

An unconditional order or promise to pay an amount of money, easily transferable from one person to another.
Payable either on order or to the bearer
Identity of payer, payee, amount, time of payment should be certain

Figure: Characteristics of a negotiable instrument

1.3 Essentials of a negotiable instrument

To understand the essentials of a negotiable instrument, it is important to bear in mind the purpose of such an instrument, which is that they may represent money and do all the work of money in business transactions. The concept mentioned "the most characteristic of money" as distinguished from other species of property, is the facility and freedom with which it "circulates". Anyone taking it during business need look no further than to the face of the coin and the possession of the person from whom he receives it. These are qualities which every representative of money must possess to answer its purpose effectively.

Therefore, that the first and essential requisite of being a negotiable instrument is "certainty". This means the following:

1. Certainty as to the person to make payment
2. Certainty as to the person to receive it
3. Certainty as to the time and place of payment
4. Certainty as to the conditions of liability
5. Certainty as to the amount to be paid.

1.4 Conclusion

In this chapter, we introduced the concept and definition of negotiable instruments, emphasizing their role in financial transactions. Understanding these foundational principles prepares us to explore their historical evolution and the legislative frameworks that govern them in subsequent chapters.

Chapter 2: Historical background of negotiable instruments legislation in Indian law

In this chapter we study the history of negotiable instruments, and how they came to be. Our focus here is the history in Indian law.

2.1 History of negotiable instruments

Negotiable instruments arose in the ancient world because of a need to have a secure and efficient way to conduct financial transactions in cases where physical money or gold was risky to take, such as in the case of long-distance trade using caravans travelling for many months.

The earliest usage of credit instruments, especially of promissory notes and bills of exchange, arose in different parts of the ancient world including in Mesopotamia, ancient Rome and China, where paper money was first used. Their use increased in medieval Europe, especially in city states in Italy such as Venice. Eventually they became formalized in English common law of 17th-18th century, with the bills of exchange Act of 1882 and the first usage of banknotes. With imperialism and globalization and world trade, their use gradually spread to all corners of the world including India.

2.2 History of laws relating to negotiable instruments in India

The history of law relating to negotiable instruments is applicable in India and as codified in the pre independence era, is a long one. The salient events are as follows:

a)   The 3rd Indian law commission originally proposed a draft of this legislation in 1866.

b)   After needful deliberations on this draft legislation, the draft bill was revised by the select committee.

c)   In 1879 Mr Arthur Phillips, the then law secretary and member of the Calcutta Bar, redrafted the bill. The draft was introduced in the council and was passed into law in 1881, becoming the Negotiable Instruments Act 1881 (Act No. 26 of 1881).

d)   The banking, public financial institutions and negotiable instruments laws (Amending) Act 1988 (LXVI of 1988): Through this amendment chapter XVII was inserted in the Act. It explained the provisions of the new chapter XVII in the following words:

- Where any cheque drawn by a person for the discharge of any liability is returned by the bank unpaid for the reason of the insufficiency of the amount of money of the account on which the cheque was drawn, or

- For the reason that it exceeds the arrangements made by the drawer of the cheque with the bankers for that account, the drawer of such cheque shall be deemed to have committed an offense. In that case, the drawer shall be punishable with imprisonment for a term which may extend to one year, or with fine which may extend to twice the amount of the cheque, or with both.

The provisions have also been made that to constitute the above offence:

- Such cheque should have been presented to the bank within a period of six months of the date of its withdrawal or within the period of its validity.
- The payee or holder in due course of such cheque should have made a demand for the payment of the said amount of money by giving a notice in writing to the drawer of the cheque within 15 days of the receipt of the information by him from the bank regarding the return of the unpaid cheque, and
- The drawer of such a cheque should have failed to make the payment of the said amount of money to the payee or the holder in due course of the cheque within 15 days of the receipt of the said notice.

Figure: First page of the Negotiable Instruments Act 1881

2.3 Introduction to the Negotiable Instruments Act 1881

The influence of British-era financial practices on the Indian legislative framework is profound. The Bills of Exchange Act, which governed negotiable instruments in the United Kingdom, served as a prototype for India's Negotiable Instruments Act.

The Negotiable Instruments Act 1881 is the main law in India pertaining to negotiable instruments. It was brought during British rule in India to facilitate banking and commercial transactions, between entities such as individuals and companies. The intention is to create confidence and create a legal framework for the widespread use of negotiable instruments such as promissory notes and cheques.

The Act defines the entities, characteristics, types, and regulations pertaining to negotiable instruments. It also has provisions for offenses upon breach of the obligations, for example if a cheque is dishonored.

2.4 Safeguards in the Negotiable Instruments Act 1881

In order to ensure that genuine and honest bank customers are not harassed or put to inconvenience, sufficient safeguards have also been provided in the proposed new chapter. Such safeguards are as follows:

- That no court shall take cognizance of such offence except on a complaint in writing, made by the payee, or the holder in due course of the cheque
- That such complaint is made within one month of the date on which the cause of action arises, and
- That no court inferior to that of a metropolitan magistrate or judicial magistrate or judicial magistrate of first class shall try such an offence.

2.5 The Negotiable Instruments (Amendment and Miscellaneous Provisions) Act 2002

The statement of objectives and reasons in the Negotiable Instruments Act 2002 stated as follows:

- The Negotiable Instruments Act 1881 was amended by the banking public Financial Institutions Negotiable Instruments laws (Amendment) Act 1988, wherein a new chapter XVII was incorporated for penalties in case of dishonor of cheques due to insufficiency of funds in the account of the drawer of the cheque. These provisions were incorporated with a view to encourage the culture of use of cheques and enhancing the credibility of the instrument.
- The existing provisions in the Negotiable Instruments Act 1881, namely Section 138 to 142 in chapter XVII, have been found deficient with regard to dishonor of cheques.
- Not only the punishment provided in the Act has proved to be inadequate, the procedure for the courts to deal with such matters has been found to be cumbersome.
- The courts are unable to dispose of such cases expeditiously in a time bound manner in view of the procedure contained in the act.

- The deficiency as shown above was referred and as per the recommendations of the working group standing committee on finance, the following changes in the Negotiable Instruments Act 1881 was recommended:
    - To increase the punishment from one year to two years
    - To increase the period for issue of notice by the payee to the drawer for 15 days to 30 days
    - To provide discretion to the court to waive the period of one month prescribed for taking cognizance of the case under the act.
    - To prescribe the procedure for disposing with preliminary evidence of the complainant
    - To prescribe the procedure for servicing of summons to the accused or witness through speed post or private couriers
    - To provide for summary trial of the cases under the act with a view of speeding the disposal of cases
    - To make the offences under the act compoundable
    - To exempt those directors from prosecution under section 14 of the act, who are nominated as directors of a company
    - To provide the magistrate trying an offence the power to pass sentence of imprisonment for a term exceeding one year and amount of fine exceeding 5000 rupees

- To make the Information Technology Act 2000 applicable to the Negotiable Instruments Act 1881 in relation to Electronic cheques and truncated cheques
- To amend definitions of bankers books and certified copy given in the Bankers Books Evidence Act 1891

2.6 The Amendment of 2015

The amendment of 2015 (26 of 2015) made considerable changes in the Negotiable Instruments Act. The amendment brought jurisdiction clause to the act. The amendment of 2015 also brought some changes to the definition of "cheque" by providing changes in explanation regarding electronic cheques.

2.7 Conclusion

This chapter traced the historical roots of negotiable instruments, highlighting their global origins and adaptation within Indian law. This historical perspective sets the stage for understanding the Negotiable Instruments Act of 1881, which will be discussed in detail in the next chapter.

Chapter 3: Preamble of the Negotiable Instruments Act

In this chapter, we briefly discuss the preamble of the Negotiable Instruments Act.

3.1 What is a Preamble of an Act?

The Preamble of an act in general affords a good clue to discover the plain object and general intention of the legislation. The Preamble of the Negotiable Instruments Act is very plainly worded and from the preamble the object of the act is made clear.

In the words of Chief Justice Dyer, the Preamble is a key to open the minds of the makers of the act, as to the mischief which they intended to redress [Stowel vs Lord Zouch (1797), Plowden 353 (369)].

In Kochurim versus state of Madras and Kerala (AIR 1960 SC 1080), the Supreme Court of India has held that the Preamble of a statute is the key to the understanding of it and it may legitimately be consulted to solve any ambiguity and to fix the meaning of words which may have more than one meaning, to keep the effect of the statute within its real scope, whenever it is open to doubt.

The preamble serves as a critical tool for legal interpretation. It not only reflects the legislative intent but also provides guidance when ambiguities arise in applying the Act. This linkage between intent and application reinforces the Act's role as a cornerstone of India's financial legal system.

The preamble acts as a guiding principle, reflecting the legislature's intent to promote trust and accountability in financial dealings. By framing the legislative scope, it connects abstract legal objectives with the real-world needs of commerce, bridging theoretical law with practical utility.

3.2 Object and scope of the preamble

The proper function of a preamble is to explain certain facts which are necessary to be explained before the enactments contained in the Act can be understood. In short, it contains a recital of the facts or state of the law for which it is proposed to legislate by the state, the object and policy of the legislation, and the evils or inconvenience it seeks to remedy (AIR 1960 SC 845 – 856). Hence, where is the language of the elective sections is clear and unambiguous (AIR 1981 SC 234 paras 39, 71), the terms of the preamble cannot qualify or cut down that enactment.

3.3 Text of the preamble

The preamble of the negotiable instruments act says: *"Whereas it is expedient to define and amend the law relating to promissory notes, bills of exchange and cheques; It is hereby enacted."*

3.4 Summary

In this chapter we have discussed the preamble of the negotiable instruments act 1881. The preamble offers a glimpse into the legislative intent behind the Negotiable Instruments Act. By clarifying its objectives, it lays a foundation for delving into the features and types of negotiable instruments, which we will explore in the following chapter.

Chapter 4: Features and types of Negotiable Instruments

In this chapter, we study the main features and types of negotiable instruments.

4.1 Features of a negotiable instrument

The main features of negotiable instruments are:

- Negotiability, i.e. it can be transferred any number of times from one party to another till the final payment is made.
- It confers absolute and good title to the transferee
- The holder can recover the money in his own name
- It consists of certain prescriptions

In the following subsections, we consider various types of negotiable instruments.

4.2 Promissory Note

4.2.1 Definition of a Promissory Note

A promissory note is an instrument in writing containing an unconditional undertaking signed by the maker, to pay a certain sum of money only to or to the order of, a certain person, or to the bearer of the instrument (Section 4 of negotiable instruments act).

PROMISSORY NOTE

Amount _____

                                        Place _____ Date _____

FOR VALUE RECEIVED, I/We _____ (borrower) hereby promise to pay to the order of _____ (lender) the sum of Rs _____
with interest of _____ % per year.
Payable on 10th of each month, beginning on date _____ until the full amount is repaid.
Payable at _____ (Bank or Address).

Signature

Figure: Example of a promissory note

4.2.2 Elements of a Promissory Note

Every promissory note must satisfy the following elements

- it must be in writing
- it must contain an undertaking to pay
- the promise to pay should be unconditional
- it must be signed by the maker

- the maker must be certain
- the sum payable must also be certain
- it must contain a promise to pay money and money only
- the payee must be certain

Promissory notes are described in section 4 of the Negotiable Instruments Act 1881.

4.3 Bill of Exchange

4.3.1 Definition of a Bill of Exchange

It is an instrument in writing, containing an unconditional order signed by the maker, directing a certain person to pay a certain sum of money, only to, or to the order of, a certain person or to the bearer of the instrument (Section 5 of the Negotiable Instruments Act).

BILL OF EXCHANGE

(Stamp)

                                                   Name of drawer
                                                 Address of drawer
                                                 Date

Amount ____

____ months after date, to pay to _____ (payee) a sum of Rs. ____
For value received

To
_____ Name of drawee
Address of Drawee

                                                 Signature of Drawer

Figure: Example of a bill of exchange

4.3.2 Elements of a Bill of Exchange

Every bill of exchange must satisfy the following elements

- it must be in writing
- it must contain an order to pay
- the order must be unconditional
- it must be signed by the drawer
- the drawee must be certain
- the sum payable must also be certain
- the instrument must contain an order to pay money and money only
- the payee must be certain

Bills of exchange are described in section 5 of the Negotiable Instruments Act 1881.

4.4 Cheque

4.4.1 Definition of a Cheque

A cheque is a special kind of bill of exchange drawn on a specified banker and not expressed to be payable otherwise than on demand (Section 6 of the Negotiable Instruments Act).

Figure: Example of a cheque

4.4.2 Elements of a Cheque

The cheque satisfies all the requirements of a bill of exchange and it is always drawn on a specified banker. It is intended for immediate payment but demand by the holder is necessary for payment. Every cheque is primarily a bill of exchange. So all checks are bills of exchange, but all the bills of exchange are not cheques.

A cheque resembles a bill of exchange in many aspects but differs from it as well.

Cheques are described in section 6 of the Negotiable Instruments Act 1881.

4.5 Conclusion

Each type of negotiable instrument has unique applications. Promissory notes are often used for short-term corporate financing, while bills of exchange serve as essential tools in international trade. Cheques, though declining with digitalization, remain a critical instrument in domestic banking systems.

This chapter examined the defining features and various types of negotiable instruments, including promissory notes, bills of exchange, and cheques. Building on this understanding, the subsequent chapters will delve deeper into the specific characteristics and legal requisites of each type.

Chapter 5: Characteristics of Bill of Exchange

In this chapter, we study the main characteristics and requisites for bills of exchange.

5.1 What is a Bill of Exchange

As per the Negotiable Instruments Act 1881, a bill of exchange is an instrument in writing containing an unconditional order, signed by the maker, directing a certain person to pay a certain sum of money only to, or to the order of, a certain person or to the bearer of the instrument. It is drawn by a banker and payable on demand.

A cheque is a common type of bill of exchange, but has some extra characteristics which we will discuss in a coming chapter.

Figure: A bill of exchange in Belgium, 1933. lokill, Public domain, via Wikimedia Commons

As per the United Nations Convention on International Bills of Exchange and International Promissory Notes (New York, 1988), a bill of exchange is a written instrument that has the following characteristics:

- Contains an unconditional order whereby the drawer directs the drawee to pay a definite sum of money to the payee or to his order
- Is payable on demand or at a definite time
- Is dated
- Is signed by the drawer

A bill of exchange is basically an order by one person, the drawer, to a bank or financial institution, the drawee, to pay money to another person, the payee. The drawer and the payee can be the same person, i.e. the bill can be drawn by the drawer to make the payment to themselves. The bill may be endorsed by the payee to make the payment to another party, who can then endorse it to yet another party and so on. Therefore, it can be transferred.

For bills of exchange in India, they must be stamped as per the provisions of the Indian Stamp Act 1899. They should mention the date and place at which they are drawn, mention the time and amount of payment, mention the drawee who makes the payment, consist only of money, must be an order or direction to pay the amount.

The use of bills of exchange in international trade exemplifies their significance. For instance, exporters and importers rely on these instruments to secure payments and reduce risks in cross-border transactions.

5.2 Types of Bills of Exchange

The types of bills of exchange include

- Inland bills: that are made and payable in India
- Foreign bills that are internationally valid, usually made in sets of three
- Trade bills, that are applicable for trade transactions such as selling goods on credit upon some consideration and constitute a legally enforceable acknowledgement of a debt
- Accommodation bills, that do not have any consideration and are not legally enforceable.

5.3 Applications of bills of exchange

Bills of exchange play a crucial role in reducing financial risks and ensuring smooth transactions in international trade. These instruments act as binding agreements between parties, specifying payment terms and providing assurance that payment will be made as agreed. For exporters, a bill of exchange guarantees that they will receive payment either immediately (sight bills) or at a predetermined future date (time bills). For importers, it provides a structured mechanism to manage cash flows while ensuring the receipt of goods as specified in trade agreements.

A typical lifecycle of a bill of exchange in international trade begins with the exporter (drawer) preparing and issuing the bill to the importer (drawee). The importer may accept the bill by signing it, thereby committing to pay the specified amount. This acceptance is a critical step as it legally binds the drawee to the payment terms. The exporter may then discount the bill with a bank or financial institution to receive immediate funds, transferring the risk to the institution. Upon maturity, the drawee pays the bank or directly to the holder of the bill.

For example, an exporter in India shipping goods to a buyer in Germany may issue a bill of exchange drawn on the buyer's bank. The buyer accepts the bill, confirming their obligation to pay. The exporter, needing immediate liquidity, can sell the bill to a local bank at a discount. The bank collects the payment from the buyer or their bank on the due date, completing the transaction.

This structured approach fosters transparency and trust between exporters and importers, reducing the risk of default and ensuring that both parties fulfill their contractual obligations. Furthermore, legal frameworks such as the United Nations Convention on International Bills of Exchange and International Promissory Notes provide a standardized basis for resolving disputes, making bills of exchange indispensable in cross-border trade.

5.4 Conclusion

In this chapter we have discussed the characteristics and types of bills of exchange. The bill of exchange is a cornerstone of financial transactions, with distinct characteristics and legal requirements. Having explored its fundamentals, we will now turn our attention to another critical negotiable instrument—the promissory note.

Chapter 6: Characteristics of Promissory Notes

In this chapter, we study the main characteristics and requisites for promissory notes.

6.1 What is a promissory note

A promissory note is a legal financial instrument where one party (the maker or issuer) unconditionally promises to pay a fixed amount of money to another party (the payee), either at a fixed or determinable future time or on demand. They are usually used as a legal acknowledgment of debts from the issuer to the payee. They may include provisions of interest added if the payment is not made by a specified maturity date, as well as other terms and conditions, such as consequences if the payment fails.

Promissory notes are commonly used for short term financing of companies. They are also sometimes termed as notes payable, or just note.

As per the negotiable instruments act 1881, a promissory note is an instrument in writing (not being a bank-note or a currency-note) containing an unconditional undertaking signed by the maker, to pay a certain sum of money only to, or to the order of, a certain person, or to the bearer of the instrument.

As per the United Nations Convention on International Bills of Exchange and International Promissory Notes (New York, 1988), a promissory note is a written instrument that has the following characteristics:

- It contains an unconditional promise whereby the maker undertakes to pay a definite sum of money to the payee or to his order
- Is payable on demand or at a definite time
- Is dated
- Is signed by the maker

Digital lending platforms and fintech innovations have revitalized the use of promissory notes. For example, e-promissory notes, governed by legal frameworks, are increasingly used in digital financing solutions.

6.2 Deciding whether an instrument is a promissory note

- The definition of a promissory note under section 4 of the Negotiable Instruments Act is exhaustive and excludes from the category of promissory notes, instruments which do not fall within its terms [Jethe Pakha versus Ramachandra (1892) 16 Bombay 689].
- No particular form of words is essential to constitute a promissory note. Any form of expression from which an undertaking to pay can be inferred is

sufficient. The instrument has to fulfill all the requisites of a promissory note to be called so and just because the parties describe it as a promissory note does not make it so [AIR 2007 Delhi 175].
- The description and language of the instrument taken as a whole, the circumstances under which it came to be executed, the intention of the parties manifest on a proper construction of the instrument determines as to whether it is a promissory note [AIR 1961 Madras 434]. A document has to be read as a whole to determine its nature.
- If there is an unconditional undertaking signed by the maker, to pay a certain sum of money only to, or to the order of a certain person, or to the bearer of the instrument, it will be a promissory note. The mere inscription of words to some effect does not determine its nature.

6.3 Characteristics of a promissory note

The characteristics of promissory notes include the following:

- They must be in writing
- They should contain a promise for payment
- The promise for payment should be unconditional
- They should be signed by the maker of the note
- The amount of payment must be fixed

- The promise to pay should include money only
- They must contain a date of payment
- They must be stamped as per the provisions of Indian stamp act 1899.
- They are legally enforceable as evidence.
- They usually specify the place where the note is made and where the payment is to be made.

6.4 Important caveats

To find out whether a particular document is a promissory note, the intention of the parties has to be looked into with reference to the substance of the document, the surrounding circumstances in which the document has been executed and its negotiability in the proper sense, whether the document was intended to be a promissory note or was intended to be a mere acknowledgement of debt or receipt of consideration.

A single instrument may embody several purposes and the document is to be read as a whole to find out its dominant purpose which is relevant for the purpose of the Negotiable Instruments Act [AIR 1968 Delhi 12].

The most important element for determination of the question whether the instrument is a promissory note is intention of the parties. If the parties had no intention to execute a promissory note, it may not be a promissory note. Thus, a document primarily intended to be receipt or a bond and not intended to be negotiable in the ordinary mercantile sense does not become a promissory note within the meaning of the act. [Lexna Krishna ji Vs Ramesh (2002) 1 BC 406].

Conversely, merely because the parties intended to execute a promissory note does not make it so, if it does not fulfill all the requirements of a promissory note [AIR 1967 Gujarat 1].

- A document which contains simply a promise to pay on demand a certain sum to a specified person is a promissory note although they may be no words of negotiability [AIR 1974 Nagpur 274].
- The mere omission of the expression "to the order of" would not render a document any the less a promissory note, if otherwise it fulfills the terms of a definition of the promissory note [AIR 1969 Kerala 188].
- The main question in deciding whether a document is a promissory note is to consider not whether it is negotiable or not but to consider whether in substance and the primary intention at the time of its execution it was a promissory note and whether it contains the necessary recitals, and is not intended to record a different kind of transaction altogether [AIR 1941 Allahabad 158].
- An instrument to be a promissory note must necessarily contain the words "to the bearer" or "to

the order". In a way the two phrases "to the bearer" or "to the order" are to be read conjugatively and not disjunctively. The sentence in the definition of promissory note that is to pay a certain sum of money only to, or to the order of, is read to be one subclause. The clear intention of the legislation is the unconditional undertaking to pay a certain sum of money only to or to the order of.

- To make a document a promissory note, it must substantially consist of a promise to pay a definite sum, and where it guarantees payment of a fixed sum on a certain date it becomes a promissory note payable otherwise than on demand.
- A document in the form of a letter acknowledging receipt of a certain sum and affixed with revenue stamp is only a receipt and cannot be termed as a promissory note.
- The definition of a promissory note in section 2.22 of the Stamp Act is wider than the definition in the Negotiable Instruments Act 1881 Section 4. If a document is not intended to be negotiable, it cannot be a promissory note in the ordinary mercantile sense [AIR 1914 Rajasthan 1].

6.5 Modern developments in promissory notes

The evolution of promissory notes continues with digitalization. Platforms now enable the issuance and settlement of e-promissory notes, governed by robust legal frameworks. This innovation simplifies processes while retaining legal enforceability, aligning traditional financial instruments with modern needs.

6.6 Conclusion

In this chapter we have discussed promissory notes and their characteristics. Promissory notes serve as a vital financial instrument for acknowledging debt and facilitating short-term financing. With a clear understanding of their features, we proceed to explore the most commonly used negotiable instrument: the cheque.

Chapter 7: Characteristics of Cheques

In this chapter, we study the characteristics of cheques, which is a widely used type of negotiable instrument.

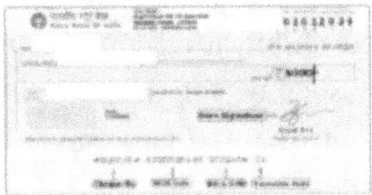

Figure: Illustration of the characteristics of cheques

7.1 Definition of Cheque

Cheque is defined as a bill of exchange drawn on a banker and payable on demand. Therefore, aside from the definition and characteristics of a bill of exchange, the cheque has two additional requirements i.e. they must be drawn on a bank and they should be payable on demand.

As per the Negotiable Instruments Act 1881, a cheque is a bill of exchange drawn on a specified banker and not expressed to be payable otherwise than on demand and it includes the electronic image of a truncated cheque and a cheque in the electronic form.

7.2 Characteristics of Cheques

The characteristics of cheques are as follows:

- As per Section 73 of Negotiable Instruments Act, a cheque must in order to charge any person except the drawer be presented within a reasonable time after delivery thereof by such person.
- The touchstone for a cheque is that it must be payable instantly on demand.
- A cheque cannot be drawn on a banker payable at a future day, that is by dating the cheque say on 1 April 1989 and be payable on a future day namely 10 April 1989. However, a cheque can be made payable on the future day by post-dating it.
- It is not required that a cheque must be drawn by a customer of the drawee bank, although for obvious reasons it is so.
- The American Negotiable Instruments Act defines a cheque as a bill of exchange drawn on a Bank payable on demand

7.3 Broader Definition and Scope of Cheques

The definition of cheque has been broadened in the Act to include the electronic image of a truncated cheque and the cheque in the electronic form. This amendment in the definition of cheque was also required to bring the Negotiable Instruments Act in tune with the Information Technology Act 2002.

Despite the amendment, the original basic definition of the cheque has been retained and the definition has only been enlarged to include in the above form as well.

Special characteristics of cheques

Always drawn on a bank or banker
Funds should be available
It is presented for payment only
Can be used as evidence of repayment of money
Has a specified validity period (3-6 months)

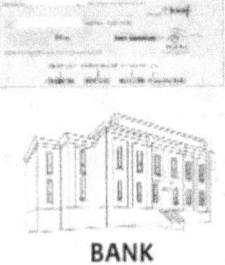

BANK

Figure: Illustration of the special characteristics of cheques

A cheque is a bill of exchange drawn on a specified banker and is payable only on demand. The necessary parties to a cheque are the same as those to a bill of exchange, save that the drawee must be a banker. The banker does not become the acceptor of the cheque, but there is an implied contract between the banker and his customer that he will honor the cheques drawn upon him by the customer up to the amount of the funds of his customer which he has in his hands, or up to the limits of amount of the overdraft agreed on. The banker's liability is to the drawer (his customer) only. The mere dishonor of a cheque gives no right of action to anyone other than the drawer (Halisbury's Laws of England).

Figure: Man signing a cheque. AI generated art by Midjourney AI

Since the cheque is a type of the bill of exchange, the definition implies that it must be drawn in accordance with the requirements of Section 5 of the Negotiable Instruments Act. No particular form of words is required, and an instrument would be a cheque if it conforms to the requisites of a bill of exchange. Accordingly, a cheque must be signed by the drawer, and must give an unconditional order to a specified banker for payment on demand of a certain sum of money or to the order of a specified person or to the bearer of the instrument.

All cheques are bills of exchange, but all bills of exchange are not cheques. A demand draft drawn by one office of a bank on another office of the said bank has been held out not to be a check. However, such a draft can be treated like a cheque for certain purposes (Section 131A of the Negotiable Instruments Act).

Figure: Man giving a cheque to a lady. AI generated art by Midjourney AI

7.4 Dictionary Meaning of Terms Related to Cheques

A cheque is a bill of exchange drawn on a specific banker and not expressed to be payable otherwise then on demand and it includes the electronic image of a truncated cheque in the electronic form [Negotiable Instruments Act (26 of 1881), Section 6A].

A cheque includes a travellers cheque [Foreign Exchange Management [encashment of draft, cheque, instrument and payment of interest) Rules 2000, Rule 2(d)]

A cheque is defined by the bills of exchange Act, 1882, section 73, as a Bill of Exchange drawn on a banker, payable on demand and generally the provisions of that act applicable to bills apply to cheques [Halisbury's Laws of England, 4th Ed, Vol 3, Para 38, Page 32].

It is an order on a bank purporting to be drawn upon a deposit of funds for the payment of a specified sum of money, on presentation to, the person named in the document, or to him on his order, or to the bearer. It is made payable instantly on demand.

Cheque book: A book containing blank cheques on a particular bank or banker with an inner margin, called a "stub" on which to note the number of each cheque, its amounts and date and the payee's name and the memorandum of the balance in bank.

Crossed cheque: A cheque is crossed for protection. The crossing is usually done by the drawer, who writes "& Co" between the parallel transverse lines across the face of the cheque, after which the cheque can only be realized by being passed through a bank. The simple "& Co" crossing is called "general". When the name of a particular bank is added it is called "special".

Cheque crossed generally: When a cheque bears across its face an addition of the words "and Company" or any abbreviation thereof (such as "& Co") between two parallel transverse lines, the cheque shall be deemed to be crossed generally [Negotiable Instruments Act (26 of 1881) section 123]

Cheque crossed specially: Where a cheque bears across his face and addition of the name of the banker, the cheque shall be deemed to be crossed specially and to be crossed to that banker [Negotiable Instruments Act (26 of 1881) Section 124]

Cheque dishonored: When the amount specified on the cheque is not paid or clearance is not given it is said that the cheque has been dishonored.

Cheque to bearer: A cheque payable to the person holding it without requiring endorsement.

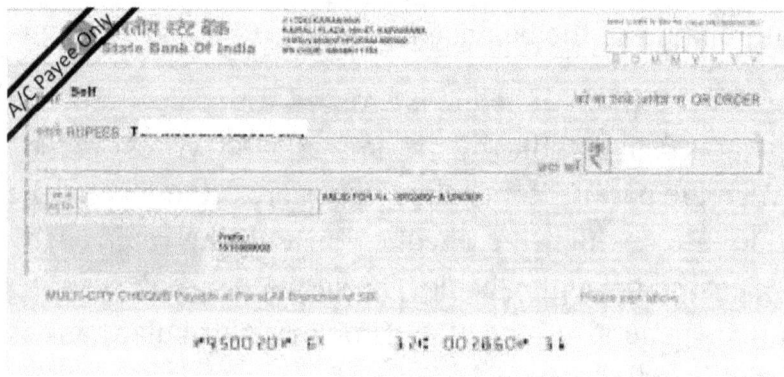

Figure: Illustration of a crossed cheque

7.5 Detailed characteristics of a Cheque

It is somewhat inaccurate to describe cheque as a bill of exchange payable on demand. While a cheque has many features in common with bills, it has several peculiar characteristics and differs from bills in some respects. Cheques are compared with and distinguished from bills as follows:

- A cheque is always drawn on a bank or a banker, and is payable immediately on demand with days of grace. [Ramswaroop vs Hardeo, AIR 1928 Allahabad 68].
- A bill of exchange is a negotiable instrument in writing containing an instruction to a third party to pay a stated sum of money at a designated future date or on demand. A cheque, on the other hand, is a bill of exchange drawn on a bank by the holder of an account payable on demand. Thus, a cheque under section 6 of the act is also a bill of exchange but it is drawn on a banker and is payable on demand. Even if a bill of exchange is drawn on a banker, if it is not payable on demand it is not a cheque. [Anil Kumar vs Gulshan Rao (1994) 79 Comp C as 150 (SC)].
- If there is no mention in the document that it is payable on demand, the said document does not fall within the definition of a cheque and it is not a cheque. The document, bill of exchange, refund order, final interest warrant do not constitute cheques within the meaning of Section 138 of the act. [Sri Vinod vs SGK Oriental 2002 (2) ALT (crl) 406 AP].

- A cheque requires no acceptance apart from prompt payment. It is presented for payment only. Accordingly, there is no privity of contract between the banker and the payee, who cannot sue the bank on dishonor of the cheque.
- A check is supposed to be drawn upon funds in the hands of the banker.
- The drawer of a cheque is not discharged by failure of the holder to present it in due time unless the drawer has sustained damage by the delay. These differences are pointed out in the well-known passage of Parke CB in the case "Ramcharan vs Luchmeechand [AIR 1944 PC 58].
- A banker's cheque is a peculiar sort of instrument, in many respects resembling a bill of exchange, but in some entirely different. A cheque does not require acceptance.
- A cheque is not noted or protested for dishonor and is generally inland; and in respect of crossed cheques there is protection given to the banker which is peculiar to these instruments.

When the Negotiable Instruments Act expressly permits and authorizes by a substantive provisions the completion of an instrument by sections 5 and 6 defining "bill of exchange" and cheque have to be harmoniously read to mean that an instrument which was initially not a cheque falling within the definition of section 6 would become a "cheque" when it was completed by filling the blanks and its dishonor shall have all the legal consequences of dishonor of a cheque [AIR 2010 (NOC) 299 Gujarat].

7.6 Pay order is also a cheque

A pay order is a cheque within the meaning of a section 138 of the act. The pay order is closer to a bill of exchange because of the unconditional order of its maker to the person concerned to pay a certain sum.

7.7 Cheque as evidence

Usually, all payments by cheque are to extinguish an existing debt, not to create a new one. Hence a cheque presented and paid is of itself no evidence of money lent or advanced by the banker to the customer. On the other hand, it is the prima facie evidence of the repayment of money previously lodged by the customer in the banker's hands, except perhaps where the cheque was paid without funds or when the payment itself creates an overdraft. Nor is a paid cheque in itself an evidence of a loan by the drawer to the payee. Yet it may be shown by other evidence that the cheque was in fact loaned to him. A cheque once drawn but not presented is not evidence of money previously lent by the drawer to the payee.

7.8 Payment by cheque

Since a cheque is not lent but it is only a means of payment, the giving of a check for an antecedent debt operates only as a conditional payment. But a cheque unless dishonored is payment when it is cleared. Payment by cheque is as good as payment in cash provided it is honored. [AIR 1966 Madras 435].

7.9 Amount to be paid by cheque

The sum directed to be paid should be distinctly expressed in the instrument both in words and figures to avoid difficulty, but either will do. If there is a discrepancy, the amount stated in words shall be the amount ordered to be paid.

7.10 Payee of a cheque

As in the case of bills, certainty of payee is a requisite for a valid cheque. But at the time of drawing, a blank space may be left so that it may be filled up by a holder to whom it may be delivered with his own name. If not so filled, it will be taken to mean payable to the drawer's order. But it may be noted that the absence of payee's name prevents its being looked upon as a cheque at all and the banker is entitled to return such a cheque for completion of the drawer.

7.11 Modern developments in cheques

The advent of electronic and truncated cheques has revolutionized traditional banking practices by introducing efficiency, security, and speed in financial transactions. These innovations significantly reduce the risk of fraud by incorporating advanced verification mechanisms, such as MICR (Magnetic Ink Character Recognition) codes, encryption protocols, and digital signatures. Electronic cheques are processed faster, eliminating the need for physical handling, while truncated cheques facilitate real-time clearing by replacing physical cheque movements with scanned images.

For example, the Reserve Bank of India's implementation of the Cheque Truncation System (CTS) has streamlined the cheque-clearing process in India. By digitizing cheque images and associated data, CTS ensures quicker settlements and reduced clearing timelines. This advancement has made banking more customer-centric and aligned with modern digital expectations.

Real-world cases, such as disputes over cheque dishonor under Section 138 of the Negotiable Instruments Act, highlight the legal implications and the role of electronic cheques in mitigating risks. One landmark case involved a dishonored cheque due to insufficient funds, where the court emphasized the importance of prompt presentation and digital trail evidence provided by the CTS. This case underscored how electronic systems add accountability and help resolve disputes more efficiently.

Moreover, these advancements pave the way for integration with other digital payment systems, such as Unified Payments Interface (UPI), to create a seamless financial ecosystem. Businesses and individuals alike benefit from reduced transaction costs, minimized human errors, and enhanced security, making electronic and truncated cheques indispensable tools in modern banking.

7.12 Conclusion

In this chapter we have discussed cheques and their important characteristics. Cheques, as a specialized form of bill of exchange, play a pivotal role in everyday financial transactions. By understanding their unique characteristics and legal requirements, we complete our discussion of the key negotiable instruments. The final chapter will consolidate these insights and reflect on their practical implications.

Chapter 8: Real-World Applications and Modern Developments

In this chapter, we discuss some real-world applications and modern developments in negotiable instruments.

8.1 Promissory Notes in Business Transactions

Promissory notes are commonly used in corporate financing. For example, when a company needs short-term capital, it might issue a promissory note to investors, promising to repay with interest within a specified period.

Case Study: An Indian IT startup, TechFlow Pvt. Ltd., needed funds for a new project. Instead of seeking traditional bank loans, it issued promissory notes to private investors. This approach allowed the company to raise funds quickly while offering a fixed return to investors. The notes were legally binding under the Negotiable Instruments Act, ensuring transparency and trust.

8.2 Bills of Exchange in Trade Financing

Bills of exchange are integral to international trade, reducing risks for exporters and importers.

Example: An Indian textile exporter sends goods to a UK-based retailer. The exporter issues a bill of exchange payable by the retailer's bank. The bank's acceptance ensures payment upon delivery, securing the transaction for both parties.

8.3 Cheques and Digital Banking

Cheques, while traditional, are adapting to modern banking through technologies like cheque truncation.

Legal Case: In the landmark case of M/S Electronics Ltd. vs. Axis Bank (2022), the court ruled in favor of the payee, emphasizing the need for timely cheque presentation under Section 138 of the Negotiable Instruments Act. The case highlighted the importance of digital systems like the Cheque Truncation System (CTS) in reducing fraud.

8.4 Digital transformation

Electronic negotiable instruments streamline processes, enhance security, and reduce fraud. Some examples are as follows:

- **E-Cheques**: An electronic cheque replaces the physical cheque with a digital image. Legal frameworks like the IT Act 2000 govern its use in India, ensuring its validity under the Negotiable Instruments Act.

- **Digital Promissory Notes**: Fintech platforms now offer digital promissory notes, enabling instant issuance and tracking.

Example: In 2023, the Reserve Bank of India (RBI) launched a pilot project integrating blockchain for e-promissory notes, reducing processing times by 30%.

Challenges and Legal Implications for digital instruments are as follows:

- Ensuring robust cybersecurity for digital instruments.
- Harmonizing laws between physical and electronic formats.
- Adapting to global standards like the United Nations Convention on Electronic Contracts.

Chapter 9: Conclusion

In this book, we have explored the definition, types, and characteristics of negotiable instruments, along with their legislative framework under Indian law. From promissory notes to cheques, each instrument serves a unique purpose in facilitating financial transactions. By understanding these instruments and their legal implications, readers are better equipped to navigate the complexities of financial and commercial dealings.

As digital technologies like blockchain and electronic contracts emerge, the future of negotiable instruments will likely integrate these innovations. Instruments such as e-cheques and smart contracts promise faster, more secure transactions. Providing businesses and individuals with guidance on leveraging these technologies responsibly will ensure the continued relevance of negotiable instruments in the modern economy.

Glossary of Key Terms

This glossary provides definitions of key legal and financial terms used throughout this book.

Acceptance: The act by which the drawee of a bill of exchange signifies agreement to pay the bill as ordered, usually by signing the face of the bill. Once accepted, the drawee becomes the acceptor and is primarily liable for payment.

Bearer: The person who physically possesses a negotiable instrument payable to bearer. A bearer instrument can be transferred by mere delivery without endorsement.

Bill of Exchange: An instrument in writing containing an unconditional order, signed by the maker (drawer), directing a certain person (drawee) to pay a certain sum of money to, or to the order of, a certain person (payee) or to the bearer. Defined under Section 5 of the Negotiable Instruments Act 1881.

Cheque: A special form of bill of exchange drawn on a specified banker and payable on demand. Defined under Section 6 of the Negotiable Instruments Act 1881. A cheque must always be drawn on a bank and is not expressed to be payable otherwise than on demand.

Cheque Truncation System (CTS): A system introduced by the Reserve Bank of India to digitize the cheque-clearing process. Physical cheques are scanned and the electronic image is transmitted for clearing, reducing the time and cost of cheque settlement.

Dishonour: The refusal by the drawee or acceptor to accept or pay a negotiable instrument when duly presented. A cheque is dishonoured when a bank returns it unpaid, typically due to insufficient funds, a stopped payment, or a closed account. Dishonour of a cheque is an offence punishable under Section 138 of the Negotiable Instruments Act 1881.

Drawer: The person who creates and signs a bill of exchange or cheque, ordering the drawee to pay a specified amount to the payee.

Drawee: The person or financial institution directed by the drawer to pay a specified amount. In the case of a cheque, the drawee is always a bank.

Endorsement: The act of signing the back of a negotiable instrument for the purpose of transferring it to another party. The person who endorses the instrument is called the endorser, and the person to whom it is transferred is the endorsee. Endorsement is governed by Sections 15–20 of the Negotiable Instruments Act 1881.

Holder in Due Course: A person who takes a negotiable instrument in good faith, for value, before its maturity, and without notice of any defect in the title of the person from whom he received it. A holder in due course acquires a good title even if the transferor's title was defective. Defined under Section 9 of the Negotiable Instruments Act 1881.

Maker: The person who creates and signs a promissory note, thereby promising to pay a specified sum to the payee. In the context of a bill of exchange, this term refers to the drawer.

MICR (Magnetic Ink Character Recognition): A technology used in banking to facilitate the processing and clearance of cheques. Characters on the bottom of a cheque are printed in special magnetic ink that can be read by automated machines, reducing errors and speeding up processing.

Negotiable Instruments Act 1881: The principal legislation in India governing negotiable instruments. Enacted during British rule (Act No. 26 of 1881), it defines and regulates promissory notes, bills of exchange, and cheques, and prescribes penalties for their dishonour.

Payee: The person to whom a negotiable instrument is made payable. The payee's name must be clearly specified in the instrument for it to be valid.

Promissory Note: An instrument in writing (not being a bank-note or currency-note) containing an unconditional undertaking signed by the maker, to pay a certain sum of money only to, or to the order of, a certain person, or to the bearer of the instrument. Defined under Section 4 of the Negotiable Instruments Act 1881.

Section 138 (NI Act 1881): The section of the Negotiable Instruments Act that makes the dishonour of a cheque a criminal offence. It provides for punishment of imprisonment up to two years, a fine up to twice the cheque amount, or both, subject to procedural conditions being met (such as presentation within validity, issuance of a demand notice, and filing of complaint within the prescribed time).

Transferee: The person to whom a negotiable instrument is transferred by endorsement or delivery. A bona fide transferee for value who takes the instrument without notice of any defect in title acquires a good title.

Truncated Cheque: A cheque that is truncated during the clearing cycle. Instead of moving the physical cheque between banks, a scanned image and data are transmitted electronically. This process, enabled under the Cheque Truncation System, speeds up clearing and reduces physical handling costs.

UPI (Unified Payments Interface): A real-time payment system developed by the National Payments Corporation of India (NPCI) that enables inter-bank transactions via mobile platforms. While not a negotiable instrument itself, UPI is part of the broader digital payment ecosystem that is increasingly integrated with traditional instrument-based banking.

About the author

Siva Prasad Bose is an electrical engineer by profession. He is currently retired after many years of service in Uttar Pradesh Power Corporation Limited. He received his engineering degree from Jadavpur University, Kolkata and has a law degree from Meerut University, Meerut. His interests lie in the fields of family law, civil law, law of contracts, and any areas of law related to power electricity related issues.

Other Books by Siva Prasad Bose

Introduction to Wills and Probate

Senior Citizens Abuse in India

Introduction to Marriage Laws in India

Neighbor Problems in India and what to do about them

Delays in Court Cases in India

Self-Publish Books and E-Books in India

Introduction to Patents and Patent Law in India

Introduction to Property Law in India

www.ingramcontent.com/pod-product-compliance
Lightning Source LLC
Chambersburg PA
CBHW070501220526
45466CB00004B/1919